THE FARMER

Anne Civardi
Illustrated by Stephen Cartwright

Designed by Roger Priddy

Reading Consultant: Betty Root
Reading and Language Information Centre
Reading University, England.

DAISY
FIELD

PERCY
PLOWMAN

HARRY

MAGGIE

PADDY

CONNIE
CLUCK

JOE
GREEN

SPARKY

THE
FARMER

THE
TRACTOR
DRIVER

THE
HERDSMAN

THE
DAIRY
WOMAN

THE
PIG MAN

THE
POULTRY
WOMAN

THE
VEGETABLE
MAN

Daisy Field is a farmer.
She lives with her family at Blossom Farm.

2

At Blossom Farm, Daisy has a herd of cows.
They give her lots of milk each day.

Her chickens lay fine
brown eggs.

And Daisy has some
big fat pigs.

3

Daisy's husband is called Bob.

Her children are called Bess and Billy.

When is the show?

It's at two o'clock

Today there is going to be a show in Farmer Black's field. Daisy tells Bob all about it.

4

After breakfast Bob goes off to work.

Bess goes off to ride on Chips, her pony.

Billy is going to help his Mum. Sparky goes too. There are lots of things to do before the show.

First they must fetch Elsie, the cow, from the field.
And get her ready for the show.

On the way they meet Percy Plowman.
He gives them a ride in his trailer.

Harry, the herdsman, looks after Elsie.
He makes sure she gets plenty to eat each day.

Elsie is Daisy's very best cow.

Daisy hopes she will win a prize at the show.

Daisy puts a long rope around Elsie's neck.
She is going to take her back to the farmyard.

Sparky decides to chase after a cow.
It makes Harry, the herdsman, very cross.

Billy catches Sparky and gives him a smack.
He has been a naughty dog.

On the way to the farmyard, Billy sees Percy.
Percy asks Billy to help him load the hay.

Billy and Sparky jump into the trailer.
Percy drives them across a big green field.

Billy helps Percy load the hay on to the trailer.
It is hard and hot work.

When they have finished they go and help Daisy.
She is having trouble getting Elsie to move.

Daisy stops at the dairy to talk to Maggie.
Maggie has just finished milking the cows.

Billy helps Maggie wash down the cow parlour.

He thinks it is fun to squirt the water.

Poor Maggie is soaking wet. She chases Billy and trips over the hose.

Billy runs and hides
behind the henhouse.

Connie Cluck is feeding
the chickens.

Billy helps Connie
collect ten big eggs.

Connie is going to take
them to the show.

Next Daisy and Billy see Paddy the pigman. He is getting Porker, his best pig, ready for the show.

Daisy sees Joe Green at the Blossom Farm Shop.
He is going to take some vegetables to the show.

Elsie is very hungry. She eats six of Joe's apples.

Joe closes his shop. It is time to go.

He loads his vegetables on to a barrow.

And he follows Daisy and Billy back to the farmyard.

Just before lunch, Bob and Bess come home.
They are going to help Daisy at the show.

First they all help to get Elsie ready. They wash and
brush her coat until it shines.

Joe, Paddy and Connie are ready to go.
But Porker wants to eat Joe's best green cabbage.

It is 2 o'clock, time for the show. It will not take long
to get to Farmer Black's field.

19

Elsie is not the only cow in the show. Judge Bean has come to choose the best one.

Porker is very bored. He is waiting to be judged.
He wanders off to find something to eat.

Elsie wins first prize. She is the champion cow.
Judge Bean gives her a big red and blue rosette.

Joe Green wins first prize too. His cabbage is the
biggest and the best in the show.

But Porker wins second prize. He thinks his rosette looks good enough to eat.

Connie Cluck gets a big surprise. One of her best brown eggs has just hatched.

The show is over. Blossom Farm has done well.
Daisy is very pleased with all their prizes.

First published in 1986. Usborne Publishing Ltd, 20 Garrick Street, London WC2E 9BJ, England. © Usborne Publishing Ltd, 1986.